TRAUMA
TO
PEACE

Mindfulness For Veterans

by
Brock Travis, PhD

Trauma To Peace
Mindfulness For Veterans
by Brock Travis, PhD

Manufactured in the United States of America

Author: Travis PhD, Brock.
Title: Trauma To Peace, Mindfulness For Veterans

Identifiers: ISBN 9781083067708

Conceptual Translator and Editor—Angie Young
Interior and cover design by Kenneth E. Bingham

For my friend Bob
who went to Vietnam
so I did not have to.
I want to thank you
for your service.

—*Brock*

—Contents—

—Acknowledgments—

I need to thank some dear friends:

Ed Lynch of Advanta Videography for filming the M4V videos.

Angie Young of Young Waters Studio for converting the videos into a book.

Pamela Phillips of Awakening Community Institute for talking this thing through.

Bonnie Rose of Ventura Center of Spiritual Living for hosting the classes.

The many veterans who have taught me about the healing of trauma.

And thanks to Joe R. for digitalizing the diagrams.

I want to thank you for your service.

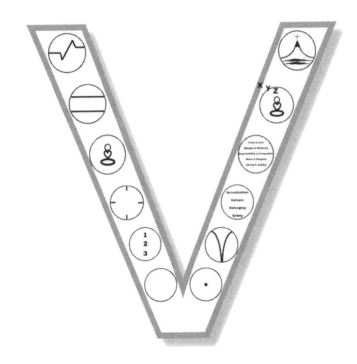

—FOREWORD—
BY
BROCK TRAVIS, PHD

SEVERAL YEARS AGO A VERY NICE LADY CALLED ME on my way out of the house, "We want you to teach mindfulness for veterans."

I said, "You know, I'm not clinical anymore."

She said, "I know, I read your website."

I said, "You know, it's spiritual now."

She said, "I know, I read your website."

I said, "Who did you say you were with?"

She said, "The VA."

I said, "Veterans Affairs wants me to teach mindfulness meditation for traumatized veterans!?!"

She said, "Yes."

This is a lot of miracles. I had been personally meditating since I was fourteen. Mindfulness had crossed my professional screen in psychology, and I had thought, "This is going to be important." So for almost thirty years I had researched and studied, practiced and taught mindfulness for schools, churches, colleges, rehabs and clinics. People would say to me, "Why are you so into that? Nobody cares about that." And finally the US federal government realizes that mindfulness can help heal trauma, even the trauma of combat and assault.

The morning of the first class I awoke from a dream. Someone had been saying to me, asking me, "What if trauma is not only a psychiatric disorder? What if trauma is a spiritual crisis?" So that evening I presented this question and that was the beginning of our journey together—Mindfulness for Veterans, or M4V.

I told the students that I was not acting as a psychotherapist treating them for post-traumatic stress disorder, but as a meditator inviting them into my own lifetime practice, the practice of mindfulness meditation. I told them that there would be just one rule for the class: mindfulness, awareness of the group and consciousness of one's self; and that we would be discussing spiritual principles, but that we would avoid political or religious arguments through honor and respect. I also informed them that I had no military experience, but I did understand trauma.

I had long felt that part of my job serving wounded warriors was to help them resolve the crippling sense of guilt some carry for the part they may have played in harming others. Fires, floods and quakes can cause trauma. But the trauma of murder, rape and torture, losses caused by other people, tends to be worse. And the people who believe themselves guilty of playing a part in causing suffering for other people can themselves suffer for decades.

It is important to realize that psychopaths are not bothered by guilt. Only a moral person is troubled by such trauma. Currently twenty-two military veterans commit suicide every day.

I would tell the vets taking my class, "You were trained to do it. You were ordered to do it. If you hadn't done it, then the other person would have done it to you and you wouldn't be here today." But the people I was working with weren't having it. They would not let me let them off the hook.

So I threw out a challenge. I drew a circle on the white board and made a little black mark in the center of it. The circle symbolizes the unity and wholeness of our being, our humanity. The dot represents a wrong-doing, some action, either one that we have done, or one that has been done to us. Whatever it is that has broken our sense of unity and wholeness. The challenge was this: "Is it possible to come to peace with a wrong?" I was asking the group to confront the things they all wanted to avoid.

The response was very serious. We sat with this riddle for weeks. Gradually a consensus emerged: One can never get away from, or get rid of a wrong, once done. But there is always a way to do the right thing. No matter what has happened. Whatever harm one has perpetrated or experienced, the potential to help others remains limitless. We may not have the power to right the wrongs of our history, but there is no end to the service we can bring into our future. This is a way to peace from trauma. *We can find purpose and meaning in whatever it was that we did or whatever it was that was done to us. And we can then find a way to bring our own moral wounding into service to others.*

The people I teach in the M4V class all have one thing in common. Some of them were officers, some of them were enlisted, some of them were in combat, and some of them were on base. Some of them have hurt other people. Some of them were hurt by other people. And some of them helplessly witnessed horrors. But all of them have found something in this world worth giving their lives for. Perhaps a cause or a friend, but something greater than themselves. These are moral people. That is why they suffer. That is also how they awaken.

The quest for recovery from trauma, whether PTSD, Military Sexual Trauma (MST), or even Traumatic Brain Injury (TBI) and other physical injuries, is a spiritual journey. As youth we tend to enter the world with a naïve childish faith: good things happen to good people and bad things happen to bad people. But some of us are forced to confront the reality of war, and the old faith is broken. Bad things can happen to me. And I can do bad things too.

The hero's journey, the warrior's journey, leads us to an awakening and a new faith:

"Whatever wrong things have been done, I can still do the right thing."

If we can come to terms with the actions that have wounded us, then these most painful, shameful, traumatizing moments of our lives can actually become a deep source of strength, a motivating force for service. This way the very darkness of the black dot drives the healing of the circle.

———

Brock Travis, PhD, serves as a meditation instructor and spiritual counselor in the Ojai/Ventura, California, area. For more information, visit www.brocktravis. com.

Reprinted with permission from The Moon Magazine.

—INTRODUCTION—

This book teaches an approach to recovery from trauma. That approach developed from an encounter between a mindfulness teacher and a group of veterans. Together they found a way to recover from trauma. That way was the practice of mindfulness.

This is not a cure, but a path.

With trauma, the body is shocked, the heart goes numb, and the mind starts flashing. With practice, we can quiet the body by sitting and breathing. We can calm the heart by feeling our feelings. And we can clear the mind by watching our thoughts. With practice, we can find a presence of loving wisdom and a greater spaciousness.

This approach is simple, but it is not easy. Trauma is a moral wounding in which we learn that wrong things can happen to us and that we can do wrong things. Recovery is a moral healing in which we find purpose and meaning in whatever happened, and put it into service for others. This journey takes courage.

We, the veterans and the teacher, have practiced mindfulness together for over four years, and at this point, we have, each of us, found some peace with ourselves. We believe that our simple approach can help others, both veterans and civilians, who seek a path of recovery from trauma. We offer it with the wish that all who need it may find some peace.

JOURNEY

SHADOWS TO SPIRIT

—Chapter 1—
Journey

SHADOWS TO SPIRIT

The morning of the first class, I woke from a dream, and someone had been asking me, what if trauma is not just a psychiatric disorder? What if trauma is a spiritual crisis? That evening, I went to class and posed those questions. What if trauma is not just a psychiatric disorder? What if trauma is a spiritual crisis? People seemed to resonate with this concept, and so we began our Mindfulness for Veterans journey together.

We started out discussing trauma as a crisis, a crossing, or a journey. It is actually a moral awakening. People come into youth with a childish, naïve morality where good things happen to good people, and bad things happen to bad people. Then, somewhere on the journey, we encounter combat, assault, or some other traumatizing factor, and the naïve childish morality is broken. We find out that good things can happen to bad people, and bad things can happen to good people. As a matter of fact, we find out that bad things can happen to us, and that we can do bad things, too. The old morality is gone, and we need a new morality.

You're going along at normal level, and something takes you down into the realm of shadows. You have to find your way from the realm of shadows to the realm of spirit. Then, you have to return, but you don't return at the same level. You return at a higher level. That is the hero's journey, or what we call the warrior's journey. The old morality is broken – good things happen to good people, and bad things happen to bad people – so we find ourselves traumatized. That is only the middle of the journey; it is not the end because a new morality is possible – a warrior's morality, a mature morality – whatever has been done, whatever I have done, or whatever has been done to me, I can still do the right thing. That is the journey.

From that journey comes a faith that cannot be taken, no matter what is happening. You can do the next right thing, the next right thing, and the next right thing. I believe this is what makes recovery from trauma possible. What I discovered in the Mindfulness For Veterans class—the veterans that I'm working with, the men and women—is that they've all come to a point in their journey, at which they've decided there is something in the world that is worth giving their life for. It might be a cause; it might be a friend, but it is something greater than one's own self.

The moment one finds there is something worth giving one's life for is the moment one becomes a warrior.

That strength is what makes it possible for us to make it all the way across this journey.

———

—Veteran Joe R.—

Seven years ago, seeking assistance with health issues
with veterans, I became aware that many things had
occurred to me in Vietnam...exposure to dioxin,
Agent Orange, and such, was doing a number on my
body. Within a couple years, the issue of not being
able to sleep, anger issues —explosive—led to psycho-
therapy.

The psychiatrist, at one point, made it clear I was suffering from PTSD, but I refused to accept that. Then,
it was suggested I attend a meeting with some other
veterans and hear about mindfulness, so I did. I was
willing to try anything at this point. As I said, I could
not sleep. I had anger issues and a constant banter in
my head that never went away. It was a totally frus-
trating experience that made it impossible to concen-
trate on an individual thing.

At the first or second meeting, during the course of
a short meditation, a suggestion was made to think
about an image, an image that would be somewhat
peaceful. The image that came to mind was holding
my grandson for the very first time. Lo and behold,
bringing that image to mind immediately stopped
the craziness that had been going on in my brain. For
the very first time in many many years, the craziness
was quiet. The hook was set, and I have been coming

back for years because you guys (veterans) continue to pique these little things that make it better.

Trauma

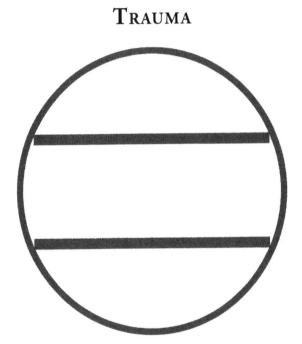

MIND IS FLASHING
HEART IS NUMB
BODY IS SHOCKED

—CHAPTER 2—
TRAUMA

BODY IS SHOCKED
HEART IS NUMB
MIND IS FLASHING

I THOUGHT THE MINDFULNESS FOR VETERANS class would last about six months, and we would spend most of it just doing basic mindfulness, focusing on the breath and the like.

That didn't happen.

A conversation developed. People who were coming to the class, and are still coming, demanded more reality and more depth, so at one point, I put the classic symptoms of trauma on the white board, and a lot happened. Seeing it in black and white made the reality come to life.

TRAUMA SYMPTOMS

The classic symptoms of trauma are hyperarousal, which includes insomnia, irritability, and hypervigilance, so I put those on the board.

The next level of trauma symptoms include avoidance. Avoiding anything that triggers a reaction. You don't want to talk about it. You don't want to look at it, and you definitely don't want to go there because it might trigger a reaction. In extreme cases, you end up feeling like you're living in a fog or living in a dream, and that's called derealization or depersonalization, where you actually feel like maybe the world isn't real, or you're not real. That is avoidance.

The next level of trauma symptoms is re-experiencing. Re-experiencing is a tendency of traumatized people to relive the traumatizing experience, and that might be memories, nightmares, and/or flashbacks.

Those are the classic symptoms of trauma: hyperarousal, avoidance, and re-experiencing. After I put the classic symptoms of trauma on the board, and while we were looking at the symptoms, I suddenly had a realization that the hyperarousal symptoms are mostly physical, the avoidance symptoms are mostly emotional, and the re-experiencing symptoms are mostly mental.

We looked at the symptoms over several classes, and they became a cornerstone of our class. We bring it back every few weeks. Our discussion gives us a deeper sense of what is happening with trauma.

On the white board, we could see the connection.

What is really happening with trauma is that the body is shocked. The nerves are shocked. The heart goes numb. The mind starts flashing.

With the body shocked, heart numb, mind flashing, I began to see the logic of it. If something occurs that is so horrific that our nerves can't stand it, we shut down our heart and our mind goes to a really weird state.

I started thinking that trauma affects us in three ways: physically, emotionally, and mentally. So if the problem is physical, emotional, and mental, then the solution would also be body, heart, mind.

If the problem develops after the body was shocked, which causes the heart to go numb which causes the mind to start flashing, then the solution would be to re-connect body, heart, and mind.

TRAUMA	SYMPTOM	SOLUTION
Body Shocked	Physical	Quiet Body
Heart Numb	Emotional	Calm Heart
Mind Flashing	Mental	Clear Mind

—Veteran Chuck R.—

I was a grunt in Vietnam. I was on the field every
night. There were ambushes every night. Trauma is
something I dealt with every day. Guys getting their
legs blown off. Guys getting their stomachs torn apart.
People dying. It is a trauma that's embedded in my
brain. Sometimes I classify myself as a prisoner of war.
I was never captured, but this trauma never goes away.

When I got back from Vietnam, I didn't have any of
this support. I found a way of hiding it all, a way of
camouflaging it. It was drinking and drugging. I did
it every day, first thing in the morning until the last
thing at night when I passed out. I drank. I drugged
every kind of drug there was. I did that for 18 years.
Then, my escape was going to be either I kill myself
and end it all, or I get some help.

I didn't kill myself, obviously, but I did start in the AA
program. There I realized I was trying to kill the pain
with drugs and alcohol. Today, I am learning how to
live and feel these pains. Today I am very thankful I
can feel them. If I can't feel what my mind and my
heart is saying, then I'm not alive. I'm dying.

AA worked for me really well for a while. Then I started going to church, and that worked for a while. Then
I started going to yoga, and that worked for a while,
but nothing really helped. My PTSD, my traumas

came back every night. They wouldn't go away.

Then, five years ago, my trauma escalated to a point where I woke up in the middle of the night, and I was hitting my wife, listening to her scream. At that point, I said I've had enough, and I started searching for real solutions.

The first thing the VA wanted to do was put me on antidepressants. I said, "No, I don't want any kind of drug. I want to be able to feel what I'm feeling and what I'm thinking."

They started getting help for me. I started going through different programs, and finally I came here and I found Dr. Brock's Mindfulness For Veterans. I started feeling those feelings, and I started welcoming those feelings.

"Come on, I want all the feelings I can have." I'd tell myself.

I wanted to remember everything now instead of forgetting. The memories started coming back to me. Reliving those things is a healing process that I can feel, and I'm so thankful to have those. I can hold my grandchildren today and love them, and feel and experience it. Thanks.

HEALING

MIND IS CLEAR
HEART IS CALM
BODY IS QUIET

—CHAPTER 3—
HEALING

BODY IS QUIET
HEART IS CALM
MIND IS CLEAR

I REALIZED NOT EVERYONE IN THE ROOM was meditating every day. Some of them probably weren't meditating except in the class. I didn't struggle with that at all. I just allowed it to be what it was. If people meditate ever, it is better than not doing it at all. I didn't try to force people to have a daily practice.

I did, however, throw a challenge. The challenge was that at some point, you decide how often, you decide when and where, but at some point find a bench or a rock, maybe overlooking water, maybe among trees.

Find a bench or a rock and sit.
People asked, "How long should I sit?"
I said, "I don't know. A while. Sit for a while, but sit fiercely. Sit with purpose. Realize that you are sitting with intention. I call that *sitting fiercely*."

13

SITTING FIERCELY

Basically, what you are doing is sitting and breathing. After you have found a place where you are comfortable, the next thing you do is to sit. While you are sitting, focus on your breathing. This will quiet the body, just to sit and to breathe. Let everything else do whatever it is going to do. You are just sitting and breathing and your body becomes quieter.

CALM THE HEART

Next is to feel your feelings because this will calm the heart. The heart calms by feeling the feelings, not by fighting them. We are not fighting our feelings. We are not trying to fix them. You are feeling your feelings. If you don't like your feelings, then try holding your heart in kindness.

WATCH THE THOUGHTS

Next is to watch the thoughts. We are not fighting the thoughts. We are not trying to fix them. We are simply watching them. If you don't like your thoughts, you can watch your mind for wisdom. Notice if your thoughts are crazy; that is good to know. Notice if your thoughts are peaceful; that is also good to know.

SITTING, FEELING, WATCHING

We sit.

We breathe.

The body gets quieter.

We feel the feelings with kindness.

The heart gets calmer.

We watch the thoughts with wisdom.

The mind gets clearer.

Sitting, feeling, watching, very simple.

Those are the givens: the body, the heart, and the mind. Those are the givens of human life. They are the proper focus of meditation.

We are not fighting ourselves. We are being present with ourselves. As far as the body goes, we are breathing the breath. As far as the heart goes, we are feeling the feelings. As far as the mind goes, we are watching the thoughts. This is powerful. We are making it very simple. We are focusing on body, heart, mind, breathing the breath, feeling the feelings, watching the thoughts. How long? A while. You are actually sitting your way toward peace.

———

—VETERAN TONY S.—

I think all of us have experienced our emotions. I get
emotional when I talk. We have all experienced the
same symptoms, like being isolated, not being able
to sleep, your mind running 100 miles an hour…
thinking that you're okay, but knowing that you're
not. I tried to suppress everything with drugs and
alcohol, but it didn't do any good. I realized there was
something better for me and my family, by bettering
myself.

At first when I came to Mindfulness For Veterans,
I didn't really buy into meditation. I didn't think it
would work for me. Nevertheless, I started trying
it for myself. I started realizing that if I cleared my
mind, if I kept myself close, that I could overcome
these things. I realized with my anger issues, I had
to keep calm in my heart and relax. I had to find out
more about myself, and why these things were happening.

I realized by meditating, relaxing, and getting to know
a little bit more about myself, I could control some of
my behavior.

By me helping others, and others helping me, we can help you the same way, by giving our own testimony. I know we have all had the same issues, and we have all worked towards getting better. I want to thank all of you for helping me.

PRACTICE

LIGHT & LOVE
ILLUMINATION & INTEGRATION
WITNESS & BEFRIEND

LIGHT & LOVE
ILLUMINATION & INTEGRATION
WITNESS & BEFRIEND

MINDFULNESS IS A PRACTICE OF CONSCIOUSNESS. We are practicing attention, consciousness, and awareness. Really, it is focus training. It is very old. It has been around forever. It is not just Buddhist. It is also in the Bible.

PRACTICING CONSCIOUSNESS

Practicing consciousness is not about going to the happy place. It is about practicing consciousness of the givens. We have a body, we have a heart, we have a mind, there are other people, and there is the world. We are bringing our consciousness first to our self.

It is important to conceive of the powers of consciousness. Consciousness has the power of light, and wherever I shine my focus, it is illuminated. Consciousness has the power of love, and whenever I hold something in my focus, it is integrated. By becoming conscious of myself, I illuminate myself and I integrate myself. This is where the learning happens and when the healing happens.

This practice is called mindfulness, but it could also be called heartfulness.

I am witnessing. I, the consciousness, am witnessing the experience of my body, my heart, and my mind, but I'm also befriending my body, heart and mind. I am observing myself, but I am also embracing myself. By knowing ourselves and by loving ourselves, we come to peace with ourselves.

That might seem a little strange, but it is important that it is not just mindfulness. It is also heartfulness. I am looking at myself, and I am feeling myself. It is by looking and feeling that I allow my whole self into consciousness. As I become aware of my whole self, this is the awakening. That is what accomplishes the healing, and that is what accomplishes the learning.

———

—Veteran Doug D.—

Illumination and integration, they sound somewhat technical. The lessons that we have picked up here allow us to approach the world from a slightly different stance than where we were coming from, and I love the idea of action and vision.

What I've tried to do with these lessons is to use them in teaching others. My target has not been grey hairs like most of us, but children. I have been so fortunate to be surrounded by grandchildren. The point I want to make is that these lessons, body, heart, mind, vision, consciousness, breathing deep, and going inside, can be received by children.

I have a 5-year-old and a 7-year-old. When I sit down with them and draw a circle, and I say, "Boys, what are we going to talk about today?"

They say, "Consciousness. Right?"

They get it. The beauty of what we have learned, and we are coming from an entirely different perspective than children, is the simplicity is there for everybody. It does take practice, and it does take focus, but the tools are all there.

ENERGY

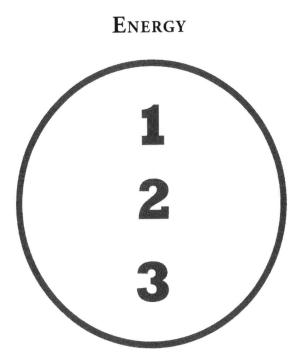

FEAR ANGER GRIEF
PANIC RAGE DESPAIR
ANXIETY IRRITABILITY DEPRESSION

FEAR ANGER GRIEF
PANIC RAGE DESPAIR
ANXIETY IRRITABILITY DEPRESSION

I'VE BEEN PRACTICING MEDITATION and mindfulness for decades, and I've been struggling with traumatic reactions for decades. However, I have realized if a person wishes to recover from trauma, he or she needs to know it and actually study it. This is a radical move because if you are having a traumatic reaction, you want to get rid of it or get away from it, but the mindfulness move is to go toward it, to focus into it, to get to know it, to study it, to observe it and embrace it. I am not saying it is easy but it is very powerful because you begin to realize these tendencies toward these reactions are energetic. They have patterns and they have depth. For instance, anxiety, irritability, and depression are pathological symptoms of trauma, but they are rooted in our human being and are part of being human.

On another level, there is fear, anger, and grief. These are primal human responses. They are normal and they are natural, and in a sense, they are healthy. In order to be a human being in this world, you need to be able to feel fear, anger, and grief. If something is threatening you, or if you are going through a loss, you need to feel that.

Trauma moves from mind to heart to body. It is at the mental level that I have the perception of threat or loss. At this level, it is actually healthy. If someone is moving against you, it is ok to be angry. These reactions are not pathological. They are not symptoms unless they become habitual. If I am in a situation in which fear, anger, and grief are intense and prolonged, so much so, that they become my way of being or simply a habit, I will develop an emotional tendency toward panic, rage, and despair.

Fear, anger, and grief are normal and natural, but to have panic attacks, to be constantly full of rage, or to fall into despair, this is not healthy. If that is allowed to go far enough or deep enough then it becomes a physical and neurological tendency of anxiety, irritability, and depression. Fear becomes panic becomes anxiety. Anger becomes rage becomes irritability. Grief becomes despair becomes depression.

If you are willing to focus toward these issues rather than try to distract away from them, you can begin to perceive that emotional reactions are a complex of mental, emotional, and physical processes. You begin to study them energetically. You begin to see that this thought has a rhythm, and this feeling has a texture. This thought causes this feeling causing this symptom, and that thought causes that feeling causing that symptom. As you begin to know the way it works, as you begin to study it, you get some freedom.

—

—Veteran Joe B.—

I have lived with this since 1969-70. What I always
told myself was it is going to get better; it will get
better as I get older. It will go away, but that was not
the way it happened. The fear, and the anger, and
grief, they became the panic, the rage, and the despair.
Those emotions became the default so much so that I
became immobilized. It just became worse, and I went
to a really dark place. I figured there was no escape. I
hate using the word suicide, but everything became
such a weight that it started looking like a relief. It
started looking like suicide would work; anything to
make the despair and the rage go away. I didn't know
what to do with it. It felt like I was going to explode
and I felt like I was such a freak.

I know now that I can deal with the feelings. I don't
even think about those dark places anymore. I don't
have to. I can live. I can find some sublime moments.
I am able to wake up in the morning and not have
that gnawing anxiety in the pit of my stomach.
It used to be that I would wake up not remembering
my dreams, but the bedding was spread all over, and
I felt terrible, like someone had been chasing me.
Now, I wake up in the morning and just lay there. My
sheets are still on the bed. I can just lay there and look
at the day. It's good. It's nice.

I have peace at the end of the day; the fear of night is gone.

The nights were the worst. The VC and NVA liked to attack in the dark. So often, I would try to go to sleep, or at the end of the day, I would try to get some rest, but I couldn't because I was thinking about being attacked. Some nights, we knew we were going to be attacked.

I brought home that fear of the darkness, and it turned into anxiety. I would question myself, "How in God's name am I going to get some sleep?" I'd drink. I'd do whatever it took, but even then, I was just killing a few of the symptoms, which wasn't doing anything for the disease.

Since this class, I have been able to start crawling out of that hole. To come here, to be here with Brock, and the energy of this room, it has been magic.

I am 69 years old, and shoot, I have a brand new life ahead of me! It's today and it's right now!

SPACE

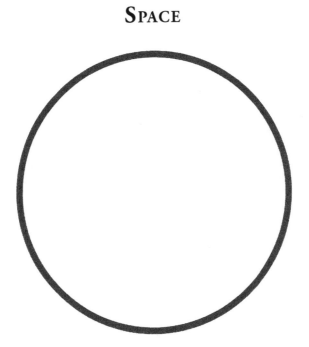

MIND & THOUGHTS
HEART & FEELINGS
BODY & SENSES

—Chapter 6—
Space

MIND & THOUGHTS
HEART & FEELINGS
BODY & SENSES

Thirty years ago I had my own trauma collapse. It wasn't due to a military experience; it was due to childhood, family, and career experiences. Basically, I couldn't eat, I couldn't sleep, and there was a lot of anxiety and depression. I had a realization. I realized that my thoughts and my feelings were crazy.

One line of thinking was saying you're fine the way you are; you don't need to learn; you don't need to heal; you don't need to grow. Everything is fine the way it is, but that way of thinking was not my friend.

There was another line of thinking that was saying you're no good; you're never going to amount to anything; people would be better off without you, and I knew that thinking was not my friend either.

I had thoughts and feelings of anxiousness and depression: craziness. Crazy means broken. Your mind and your heart are not working as a unit. They are not whole, and I was definitely having that. I know crazy is not a politically correct term, but that is how I felt.

The realization was that even if my thoughts and my feelings are crazy, I can still make wise choices and take kind actions.

Wait a minute! I thought I *was* my thoughts and feelings. But my thoughts and feelings were wrong, they were crazy, and I noticed I could still do the right thing.

This is really important. What that means is that we are greater than our thoughts and feelings. There is something about us, our consciousness, what used to be called our soul, our being, that is greater than our thoughts and feelings. This consciousness can be somewhat free of our thoughts and feelings.

Thoughts and feelings can be crazy. I don't have to be crazy. I have thoughts and feeling, but they do not rule me. I rule them.

It is not a matter of fighting them or forcing them. It is a matter of knowing them and feeling them, so I learned to bring my mind to my heart and find my breath. This was revolutionary. This was transformative.

You bring your mind to your heart and find your breath.
You feel your feelings; you watch your thoughts.

Mind your heart
Breathe your breath
Feel your feelings
Watch your thoughts

We are not fighting our feelings and we are not fighting our thoughts. There is no winning that war. There is no peace in going to war with our own being.

I'm breathing my breath; I'm feeling my feelings; I'm watching my thoughts and there's this space. Everything becomes more spacious. In this space, I am conscious of the body, the feelings, and the thoughts. By being conscious of them, I have some perspective and I have options. I am can be free of the urgings of my body, my feelings, and my thoughts. I can make good choices and take good actions no matter what.

———

—Veteran Walter K.—

Mind and Thoughts
Heart and Feelings
Body and Senses

This has meaning for all of us because we have been studying, practicing, thinking about these things for years. Most of us came here with a whole bunch of "stuff" and we focused on our "stuff." That is where we started when we began this class, focused on our "stuff."

What Brock is talking about is beyond that. What we have realized is practical. All that "stuff" is wiped out, not because it is gone, but because it is just "stuff". We have learned that there is space, and the space is what is important. Our history does not limit where we are going.

PEACE

TRAUMA

CONSCIOUSNESS

—CHAPTER 7—
PEACE

TRAUMA
CONSCIOUSNESS

In this class, and in working with other traumatized people, I thought part of my job was to help people forgive, to forgive themselves and to forgive others. I would try to urge things toward that.

In the Mindfulness for Veterans class, I was telling people, "You were trained to do that. You were ordered to do that, and you needed to do that because if you hadn't done it, then the other person would have done it to you, and you wouldn't be here today." The veterans were not having any of that.

I noticed that people in the class were struggling with guilt and shame, but they would not let me let them off the hook. They were not letting me free them from that guilt and shame that they were feeling. I respect these people and honor them, so I stopped pressing for that, but I threw a challenge.

I drew a circle on the board. The circle represents our

35

being, what used to be called the soul. It represents consciousness and then I put a little black spot in the middle of the circle. The little black spot represents the wrongdoing, whatever we did or whatever was done to us.

Then I asked this question. Is it possible to come to peace with the wrongdoing? Is it possible? You can never make it go away. You can never get away from it. It may always be there, but is it possible to come to peace with it?

The consensus from the class, from our years of dealing with this, is yes, because no matter how bad that little spot is, the potential to do good is limitless. No matter what wrong has been done, no matter what wrong I have done or has been done to me, the potential to do the right thing, the next right thing, and the next right thing, remains. This was revolutionary.

This is how recovery from trauma works. We find the purpose and meaning in whatever has happened, no matter what it was, and then we put it into service to others. This is a reliable way to recover from trauma. We can't get the little black spot to go away. We can't make the wrong not have happened, but the potential for doing right remains limitless.

—Veteran Ken B.—

I can relate to the black spot in the middle of the symbolic *Peace* diagram. One of the unfortunate—and *mean*—actions I was involved in was inadvertent and unforgettable. It happened during my second tour to Vietnam in 1968.

Returning to base-camp driving a Weapons Carrier (small truck) from a bridge project, we stopped at "Dog Patch." That's what we called small villages along the roads in Vietnam. We bought a few warm beers from one of the Vietnamese vendors. We proceeded down the road having our beers and getting a buzz.

So, we're driving along, and my so-called friend Rich, told me, "Pull over a little bit, Ken. Pull over." So I pulled over a little. Well, Rich reached over, opened the door and put his foot against it, and forcefully push-kicked the door open into an old man on a bicycle.

I was shocked. I didn't know what to do—but I didn't have the guts to stop either.

A few of the villagers were yelling and pointing at us and the old man. I don't know if we killed him. I don't know if we injured him bad, but he was an old man. I could see him in the rear-view mirror.

I had my .45 with me, and I felt like shooting Rich.
He was a rowdy guy, but he didn't have enough beer
in him to do that. I believe it was innate. Rich died
young upon returning from Vietnam. I think he had a
lot of hate in him before he even got to Vietnam.

Anyway, the black spot in the middle of the circle is
a good concrete concept for me— knowing that it is
not going to go away—and it shouldn't. I can deal
with it.

Being older and looking back, I can now understand
the patterns that led to my high scores on VA's PTSD
testing and resulting symptoms that have plagued me
for 50 years.

Personal tragedies, just prior to—and during—my
first tour to Vietnam led to heightened sensitivity and
left me vulnerable to additional traumas experienced
during my second and third tours to Vietnam.

It's Dr. Brock Travis's recent Mindfulness instructions
that have given insight to my disorder and rendered
relief from the symptoms. *Thank you Brock.*

SERVICE

VISION
PASSION
ACTION

—CHAPTER 8—
SERVICE

VISION
PASSION
ACTION

TRAUMA IS ABRUPTION. Abruption means a breaking. Actually, craziness means broken, or brokenness. What happens in trauma breaks the natural healthy connection between the body, the heart and the mind. In a healthy person, there is a natural connection between body, heart and mind.

If I encounter trauma, it could be an assault, it could be combat, some sort of threat or loss, and if the trauma is intense enough or prolonged enough, it disturbs the natural connection, which causes abruption or brokenness. It feels like craziness, and that is the problem.

The solution is alignment. If I can realign my body, my heart and my mind, then I am going to feel a sense of peace because it is a natural state for a body, heart and mind to be working as a unit, to be working as a whole. That natural state feels like peace. Even if we are in difficult or dangerous circumstances, if we feel an alignment between our physical, emotional and mental aspects, we experience that as tranquility or serenity, in other words, peace.

The problem is trauma, which is an abruption, and the solution is peace, which is an alignment.

I am discovering from working with traumatized people, and also alcoholic and addictive people, that service realigns the person. Service is a way to help heal the abruption.

How does that work?

If I have a vision of a purpose or meaning that is greater than myself, and I fill my mind with that vision, then my mind is clear. If I have a passion for a purpose or a meaning greater than myself and I fill my heart with that passion, then my heart becomes calm. If I move my arms and legs in alignment with that vision and that passion, I am actually aligning my body, my heart and my mind through action.

Service is a vision in the mind, passion of the heart and action with the body. This is the reason that service brings us to wholeness. It is the solution to the problem. The problem of trauma is abruption where we are broken apart. The solution to trauma is peace, which is an alignment of body, heart and mind. The way we do that is to put our body in service to the passion and the vision by acting upon the vision and the passion. Vision, passion, action.

———

—Veteran Edmund G.—

My personal story relates to Native American Ceremony. Prior to doing that, I was on the board of directors of a church. At the first board meeting, I knew that it was not going to be a very good match, but I stayed for my three years. During that time, I found Native America Ceremony. I took to that immediately.

We work with Earth, fire, air and water, and everybody sits at the same level. During a sweat lodge, it is dark in there, so you don't dress up to impress anybody. You just show up. That is the whole key that aligns with this concept of service. We show up to do whatever needs to be done, split wood, to keep fire. Then as you continue to show up, other people come and tell stories about their experiences at higher levels of spirituality, and you just keep on coming back.

On occasion, I question myself.

For me, I've been on this path for about 25 years, and I don't have any idea where I would be without it. I come to Mindfulness For Veterans because of the meditation information, and to learn how to deal with the situations that come up in my life. We are never going to be able to get away from situations. We just gather tools so that we can handle them better. Many people respect me, and when they get into a hard situation, they will call and ask for my advice. I pass along these 12 principles.

From practicing mindfulness, I feel much calmer. I continue to give back, and there is that warm feeling in my heart. Mindfulness is a continuation of my path of good things, good thoughts, and being of service.

ACTUALIZATION

DEDICATION
ABSORPTION
REALIZATION

DEDICATION
ABSORPTION
REALIZATION

THIS IS GOING TO SOUND a little bit psychological because it is. There were two revolutionary psychologists in the 20th century, Maslow and Rogers. They were investigating a phenomenon they called actualization. Actualization can be thought of as becoming what we were meant to be and fulfilling our potential.

Actualization has a lot to do with recovery. In a sense, actualization and recovery are the same thing. In order to achieve actualization, people need safety, belonging and esteem. Therefore if we are trying to recover from trauma, then we also need safety, belonging and esteem in order to fulfill our potential and to align the abruption.

Actualization is a little problematic in our modern world, especially in the military, but safety does not have to mean physical security. Safety can mean sureness. It can mean I am sure I am not doing the wrong thing, I am sure that I am doing the right thing. Even if I am in a difficult or dangerous situation, I might still feel serenity and tranquility because I know I am not in the wrong and know I am in the right. If I have safety, then I can move to the next level which has to do with the heart.

The next level is called belonging, and belonging is really respect. If I am able to respect myself and respect the people in my group, and if they respect themselves and they can respect me, I am going to achieve this sense of belonging. If I have belonging, I can move to the next level, which is esteem.

Esteem is really honor. If I am standing in honor and I am honoring the people in my group because they are also standing in honor, then I achieve esteem. Then I can actualize.

I have safety, which is not necessarily the lack of danger or difficulty, but knowing I am on the right path; I am not on the wrong path. I have belonging, which is really the respect for myself and others in my group. I have honor, which is a sense of my own integrity; I am honoring the people in my group for their integrity and they are honoring me for mine. Then amazing things become possible and people can fulfill their potential and they can become what they were meant to be. This is actualization.

Actualizing people share common traits, and those traits can be seen as a path. Actualizing people are dedicated to something greater than themselves, some purpose or meaning, a friend or a cause. They are dedicated and become fully absorbed. In other words, they are in the zone, in the flow of it, having a peak experience because they are so deeply engaged in what they are doing. With dedication and absorption, one will achieve realization, which is synonymous with actualization. It means that whatever I am dedicating myself to and whatever I am absorbed in will realize itself through me.

For example, let's say I dedicate myself to liberty and justice for all and I absorb myself in liberty and justice for all. Then those principles will realize themselves through me. They will come into me and into my world.

Dedication, absorption and realization—these are traits of actualizing people, and they are also a path to actualization.

In trying to recover from trauma, we must find something greater than ourselves. We dedicate ourselves to it, we absorb ourselves in it, and it will realize itself through us.

—Veteran Mike F.—

Two years ago I read a little ad in a throwaway paper in Camarillo. It was as big as your thumb, and it had to do with mindfulness for veterans. I said, "Well, what the hell." I went to the meeting and you all, plus maybe 25 other people, were there. Over the two-plus years, some came, some went, some continued to come and some continued not to come, but here we are.

What I like most about what we were doing and how we were doing it is that Brock set the rules. I did not particularly like them, but he set them nonetheless. I thought it was my job to be tolerant of these rules.

No politics; that really rubbed me the wrong way.
No religion; didn't care about that.
No commentary on what another man said; I cared about that.
No crosstalk; I cared about that.

Those rules set the direction for all of us. They were positive guidelines for our group. I have said this to several people already, but the beauty of what we have going here...and I'm saying this for me...that I probably would not have talked to any one of you as individuals going down the street, in a restaurant, in a show, at a park, but I'm glad that I stayed and I met you.

It takes fortitude to be here. I think we are here not only for ourselves but for other people so that we can give them some vision, some light, some direction. Brock is the leader, talented, educated, relatively soft spoken, and above all patient, patient with each of us and particularly me. That is what we all need. We need that guiding voice, that soft voice, that direction while leaving the side doors open so none of us feels we're in a box, if that makes sense.

For me, the images on the whiteboard made all the difference in the world on how I viewed this stuff because I am a visual guy. If I can see it, I can do it, I can build it, or I can make it. I have to see these things because the words just kind of pass by. That is what happens when you've been hit in the head too much.

Personally, in the time we have been together, I've been amazed at the progress of each one of you. It just confirms to me that we change. We can change, and we do change, and it is usually for the better. I have said it before...We are all miracles.

I've also discovered that I do man tears at my age, and it's okay. We are all heroes. We are heroes to each other. We are heroes to all of us. We are heroes to some of us, but I believe we are all heroes because we are standing here. We are doing it for our own good and to help someone else down the road by a word, or a deed, or a thought.

Again, when I first came a couple of years ago, it was mindfulness. I didn't know what it was. I thought I'd give it a chance, but when it came to meditation I said, "Oh shit. I'm out of here." Then the words that would come from the likes of a Brock because of his education and experience, the love, the light, the dun-dun-dun. What a crock of shit. But, time heals all wounds, and so here I am. Here we are.
Thank you.

PRINCIPLES

Truth & Love

Wisdom & Kindness

Responsibility & Compassion

Honor & Respect

Liberty & Justice

—Chapter 10—

PRINCIPLES

IF A PERSON IS TRYING TO RECOVER FROM TRAUMA, he or she needs something reliable to commit to. We need purposes and meanings that are worthy of service. We need the ideals to be something that will not betray us and something that will be constant. In my work with traumatized people and recovering people, I have found that the verities are reliable. The verities are the universal principles of humanity. All tribes have principles; no group endures without them. By studying human systems, globally, across millennia, and across continents, you can get a sense of the universal principles. There are many ways to put this list together, but the list I have been working with is:

Truth and Love
Wisdom and Kindness
Responsibility and Compassion
Honor and Respect
Liberty and Justice

All of these principles are reliable. If I if I dedicate my life to these and absorb myself in these, they will not betray me. They are a good foundation for integrity. They are ideals worth serving and that is important if we want to recover from trauma.

———

—Veteran Harold S.—

The first time I experienced what I found here at Mindfulness For Veterans was at a book signing, umpteen years ago, by a gentleman by the name of Ron Kovic. He wrote a book called *Born on the 4th of July*, which was about his Vietnam experience. I had heard about his story and it sounded quite interesting, so my wife and I went to the book signing. We got in the long line and of course, they were selling the book so I bought a copy. I was looking through the book and I got to page 26 where he describes what it felt like to kill another human being in such soul-wrenching terms that I was just mesmerized by the experience of reading it.

Well, the line progressed and everyone was getting their book signed. They would open the cover, and he'd sign each one. I got to the front of the line, and we had some polite conversation. I asked Ron if he would sign page 26 for me. He looked at me and at that moment there didn't have to be any words because it wasn't two people, it was like the two of us had become one person. We both cried. And certainly he signed, and I still have the book.

Well, that experience touched me in the same way as this mindfulness work with veterans has touched me. We don't necessarily have to say everything that we feel. We say who we are. It is that honor and that respect that I have come to understand. It is the authenticity; it is that touching of souls that happens within this room when we have our meetings. It is not the honor and respect for a flag or country. It is the honor and respect for what we each carry within ourselves. We honor that and we respect whatever the other has to say.

XYZ

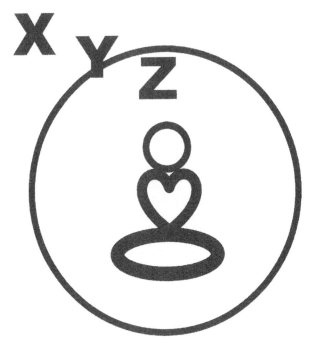

SPIRIT
CONSCIOUSNESS
MATTER

—Chapter 11—
XYZ

SPIRIT
CONSCIOUSNESS
MATTER

I WAS ASKED TO TEACH MINDFULNESS FOR VETERANS and that was very humbling for me because my neighbor went to Vietnam, but I did not go. I felt that I should be very careful in approaching this. I told the people it's not that I'm a psychotherapist treating you for trauma. I have done that, but this is not that. Mindfulness For Veterans is an invitation into the practice, of this ancient meditation, mindfulness.

During our meetings, I was trying to keep it real and actually trying to keep it 'normal' but the group demanded the reality. The truth is that the depth of this practice is mystical.

This is the way meditation heals and teaches, the why and how meditation brings about awakening.

Reality has a material dimension, or physical element,

but also reality has a spiritual dimension, the divine. The way mindfulness practice works is to awaken our consciousness to both, the material and the spiritual.

Let me lay this out like algebra, so it is logical.

- Let X be the *spiritual dimension.*
- Let Y be the *conscious dimension.*
- Let Z be the *material dimension.*

How do we bring our material life into the spiritual?

How do we bring our spiritual life into the material?

The answer is consciousness.

Through the practice of attention, consciousness, and awareness, that is how the awakening happens and that is how we recover.

I become aware that I have a body; I have a heart; I have a mind, but I am consciousness and that means I am a transcendent being. I am a spiritual being.

I am conscious that I have a body; I am conscious that I have a heart; I am conscious that I have a mind, but I am greater than these things. I am a spiritual being.

—Veteran Pat P.—

I was thinking as Brock was going through this particular lesson and diagram, that all of the diagrams and
all the lessons are critically important. What I try to
do is figure out how these concepts manifest inside of
me. The best way for me to learn and to apply what
I am learning is to see how it affects me personally. I
started that a while ago when we were going through
another lesson. Brock challenged us to ask ourselves,
"Do you know it? Or did you just read about it?"

So when we were talking about this particular diagram, I went back and spent a lot of time trying to
figure out how does this affect me personally. What
do I want to gain out of this? I knew that I was matter
and I was getting in alignment with my body, my
heart, and my mind. I was raising my consciousness,
but I was really trying to get in touch with spirit. I
grew up in a religious family and I knew what God
was, well at least I thought I did until we got to this
lesson. This lesson became so important to me because I started to meditate and practice mindfulness
and understanding, and the best way for me to try
this out was to ask questions. I started asking questions like what should I be doing with my life now?
What should I be doing to help others, if that is the
right thing for me to do? What started happening was
a connection through the consciousness, through the

soul, through the essence of who I was. I started to get little feelings and inklings that I needed to take what I was learning and start sharing it with others because I was beginning to get answers.

I, like many of you, had trauma, so I had reasons for what I was doing, but I didn't know why. So I would ask, why am I feeling this way? Why am I doing what I'm doing? Those questions were being answered. The voices, the little inklings…the feelings, much more than voices, were coming to me. I tried to put a name to it. I've talked to a lot of people about it. What started to come back was that is your intuition talking to you. That is you talking to the Universe, to the Divine, to the Beloved, and the Beloved is sharing a message with you through your guardian angels that you're calling intuition. I kept putting this into practice. I kept asking those questions. Why am I here? What am I supposed to be doing? The answer that came back was to help others be the very best they can be. You have experiences. You are a unique individual. You have value. You bring something that they can use.

One of the other answers that came back was, "So are they." They are unique and valuable. They bring a lot to the table. Listen to them. Listen to what they have to say.

After a while, I put this into practice. Now I do this with a lot of my clients. We spend some time talking about the mind, the heart, and the body. Understanding what those feelings are. Understanding what those thoughts are. Knowing that they can't hurt you and they can't kill you, but understanding where they came from is critically important and that's where X Y Z came in.

I'll get them into a place where I say, "Now, you don't have to share this with me, but why don't you ask your higher spirit, your guardian angel, your master—whoever that is, the Universe, what is it that you specifically need to learn? What do you specifically need to know? If you care to share that with me that would be great.

Some of the stories that I have heard, some of the progress that we have been able to make, the breakthroughs have all come from X Y Z. Listening to everybody, everybody has a story. Everybody has something to offer. They are all unique and valuable. You just have to ask them. That is what X Y Z does for me.

It gets me to a place where I can do that kind of stuff, and it all started with my simple meditation after Brock shared this lesson with us. I said, how do I manifest this, how do I make this real, what am I going to do with this? The answers came: You have to listen to people, help them become the very best they can be, and you, in turn, will become the very best that you can be. So, I continue this on a daily basis. I think it is extremely important. It is one of the most valuable lessons I have learned.

So again, it is so important to manifest it and put it into practice and make it real for you, and when you do, you feel it. It is a feeling that overcomes you. It is a passion that drives you. That's where I use X Y Z.

LET

THE WAY

—Chapter 12—
Let

THE WAY

EVERYTHING IN THE WORLD IS IN ACTIVITY, but not everyone in the world is in contemplation. So, it's a fierce act of will to pause and sit. Ultimately, you're going to need wisdom and kindness while you are driving, while you're talking, and maybe even while you're fighting, but this practice involves sitting. The posture should be stable and comfortable, but not rigid. If your knee hurts, move it (nobody cares). Also, it should be respectful because we're honoring the lineage all the way back to shamans and all the people who have paused from activity and entered into contemplation. I am going to ask you to pause and sit for a while.

You pause. You sit.
You settle into a posture that is comfortable and respectful.
Honoring, but not rigid, and you breathe.
Pause. Sit. Breathe.
Let the body become quiet.
Feel your feelings, whatever they are.
We're not fighting them. You feel your feelings.
Let the heart become quiet.

Watch your thoughts, whatever they are.
We're not fighting our thoughts.
You watch your thoughts.
Let the mind become quiet.
Let, not force.

Let the body be quiet.
Let the heart be quiet.
Let the mind be quiet.

There is still going to be heartbeat and breathing
and feelings and thoughts.
We don't have to get rid of those.
We don't have to get away from them.
You're not going to war with any of that.
You simply let it be and let it go.
You sit, you breathe, you feel, and you watch.
Whatever arises, as you breathe in, let it be.
As you breathe out, let it go.
As you breathe in, let it be, as you breathe out, let it go.
Just for a moment, rest in your own being.
Let yourself feel what you feel.
Let yourself know what you know.

LET.

As you move into the world again,
attend to whatever presents itself
and respond to the demands of the moment.

—Veteran Gilbert M.—

On the subject of *LET,* for the majority of my life I did not use or allow *LET* into my life. I believed I had to control everything that happened. I was taught this as a child. Whatever I was going to have, I had to create, and so I jumped on that and thought I was fairly successful. In a lot of ways, I was, but in a lot, I wasn't. There came a point in my life when everything that I thought I knew or believed in, stopped. I may as well have walked off a cliff because I thought my life was over. I didn't have a job. I didn't have a family. I didn't have a place to live. I didn't have anything and I didn't have these tools, these amazing tools to help me so I suffered for many years. I made very unwise decisions and it created chaos in my life.

Ultimately, I got into 12-step recovery, and the concept of *LET* was there. I didn't really see it like that at the time, but it was there. That started a journey to peaceful living. At the same time, I dove into American Indian Ceremony and the two of them together worked really well.

Today, I let my life be as it is. For a long time, I haven't forced anything. When the time came that I didn't want to commute to Los Angeles any longer, I just let it be and found something to do here locally. When I trust in the Creator and I trust in this concept of *LET,* things work out fairly well. I use this concept quite a bit today because it makes my life more peaceful when I let things be and when I let people be, especially people. I have to deal with people every day. We are social beings, we have families, and we experience people in all areas. Now, I allow people to be who they are, and who they aren't. There's no judgment anymore. That's just the way he is. That's just the way she is. I let it be.

In some instances, we have to socialize with family members or other people, and in a group, I may not like one or two people, but I let them be. I have a choice whether I interact with them or not.

The concept of *LET,* in almost all areas of my life, allows me to lead a much more peaceful life. It is interesting now because without judgment, I see people for what they are, and it is funny. They are who they are, and they act this way or that way.

In studying mindfulness, I have learned to understand how or why some people act as they do. Then if they ask me, I can give them this information on mindfulness, and help them. If they are suffering, I can introduce the subject of *LET.*

Like Brock said, it is difficult. I struggled with it for a long time. I didn't want to let go of my control. I thought I had to maintain control or I wasn't going to be a successful person, or a good friend, or a good parent. Now I allow everybody and everything to be. This way, I don't have any judgement. I see people, and I love them more because they are just who they are. Just that makes my life more peaceful, active and interesting.

It's a powerful concept, but for many of us we don't know how to let things be. We don't know how to let things happen.

It has been an interesting road, letting the concept of *LET* into my life. I thank Brock and all of you in this group for participating in this. To all of those out there, meditation is an awesome subject and you could really benefit from it

———

—Veteran Debora E.—

My experience is different than most of the other veterans in the class, but I have found that we do have a common bond, and part of the process is connecting with others. Just knowing that you are not alone, knowing that others have been where you've been, and have found help and feel better makes a difference. We help each other.

Forty plus years ago, I experienced military sexual trauma (MST) and for 40+ years, I kept my mouth shut. Living with the experience for so long locked inside, I began to question if I was going crazy. Coming to the Mindfulness For Veterans group has taught me how to work through this trauma.

When I practice mindfulness, I visualize my mind, heart, and body. I practice just seeing my thoughts, feeling feelings, and connecting with my body. On a regular basis, my mind, heart, and body are more balanced. If I am feeling stressed, I look for the opportunity to meditate because it helps calm me down. Afterwards, I feel refreshed and have more positive energy.

With meditation, I am safe. It wasn't always like that. Now, I am able to feel secure with my thoughts and they are safe to view and experience. There is recovery from the trauma and it is a lot better on the other side. I have found that reality is a relief.

My goal is to get people connected with the VA, and find the resources they need. I know that an individual has to engage with the program. They have to want to be involved. People like to make excuses why they can't do things, and the truth is if people aren't ready for change, then a sustained change is not likely, but if you are ready, it will work.

Any idea that is sufficiently different from your current worldview will feel threatening. And the best place to ponder a threatening idea is in a non-threatening environment. As a result, books are often a better vehicle for transforming beliefs than conversations or debates.

———

—Veteran Karina A.—

I served in Iraq in 2007, so at first it was difficult to be in this class with Vietnam veterans. I didn't feel like I belonged here, plus it was embarrassing to feel crazy or broken, but it didn't take too long to realize that even though our experiences were different, our feelings were the same.

I had tried meditation in the past, but most of the time I ended up replaying scenes from the past, and that just took me to a dark place.

Before coming to Mindfulness For Veterans, I was used to reacting to my thoughts. With mindfulness, I can sit and watch my thoughts. I don't have to react. Now I understand that I am not my thoughts. That sounds so simple, but knowing this really changed how I feel and how I react.

When something does come up, I can stop and pay attention. I am not afraid of my thoughts now because I know I am not my thoughts. It's like a door opens and I can go inward. I go deeper and try to understand.

If I am reliving something from my past, I can fast forward. I don't stay stuck. I forward to what is actually happening, and I choose to look at all the good things happening now, and know that the past is the past.

By paying attention to my body, heart, mind, it is a door into the unknown, a door to somewhere spacious where I can see the bigger picture, and in that place there is something better for me.

With mindfulness, I understand myself, and I have grown past the person I was when I was in the military. All the racing thoughts went away when I gave them the attention that they needed.

———

—Veteran Joe T.—

The reason I started going to Mindfulness For Veterans was because my doctor "suggested" it. I hated the idea, and in my usual hateful state, I told him what I thought of the idea. He kept on me to go, and finally I agreed to go, but just once. I walked in begrudgingly, not wanting to be there, but I could tell right away, that the other veterans in the class were like me.

That night Brock asked everyone to think about how they dealt with stress. We went around the room describing how we coped. Some guys were saying how they couldn't sleep, and I hadn't gotten a full night's sleep in 40 years. Then one guy told the group, "All I need is one bullet." I connected immediately.

Something else I noticed that night…some guys were saying, 'Ya, I used to be like that.'

Professionally, I got into a career where I was helping others deal with trauma. Ironically, I was not taking care of my own. There I was helping others and meanwhile my thinking was crazy. I wondered why I was always tired, angry and paranoid. I never talked about it to anyone or did anything about it until I came to M4V and found other likeminded people that had experienced what I did as a teenager. We were all experiencing the same things. Luckily, I was tired of living that way and found M4V.

Since learning this mindfulness technique, everything has changed. I use it all the time. Sometimes I forget to practice, but as soon as I realize what's happening, or what's not happening, I slow down. I stop and practice connecting my body, heart and mind.

I am a blessed person. Life has always given me gifts, and mindfulness has changed my life. I am fully aware because of meditation. People in my life have seen me change.

Another thing I have learned is how everything changes when I remind myself to be grateful. I can change my attitude with simple gratitude. I came back from Vietnam full of fear and anger. I felt betrayed. I carried all that with me, and it made me feel crazy. My thinking was way out. I had strange ideas. Being part of this group got me to look at my trauma. I am able to sleep, a deep sleep, and wake up feeling rested. I don't have to carry my past with me anymore.

One thing is certain. If I hadn't started practicing mindfulness, I would not be here now.

—GLOSSARY—

Abruption:
The sudden breaking away of a part from the whole.

Actualization *(self-actualization):*
The achievement of one's full human potential
through dedication, absorption, and creativity.

Depersonalization:
The sense that one's self is unreal.

Derealization:
The sense that one's world is unreal.

Hyperarousal:
Insomnia, irritability, and hypervigilance.

Re-experiencing:
Flashbacks, nightmares, intrusive memories.

—SITTING FIERCELY—

Find a rock or a bench

over water or among trees.

Settle into a posture that is

comfortable and respectful.

Breathe your breath.

And let your body be quiet.

Feel your feelings.

And let your heart be quiet.

Watch your thoughts.

And let your mind be quiet.

This might take awhile...

Await a moment of peace

Made in the USA
Lexington, KY
03 December 2019